BASEBALL

SCORE WITH STEM!

By Jim Gigliotti

Consultant: Tammy Englund, science educator

BEARPORT
PUBLISHING

Minneapolis, Minnesota

Credits

Cover and Title Page © Alex Staroseltev/Shutterstock; 4–5, © Focus on Baseball; 6–7, © Jon Schulte/Shutterstock; 7, © Paul Yates/Shutterstock; 8, © JoeSAPhotos/Shutterstock; 9 top © Decheve/Dreamstime; 9 bottom Cliff Welch/Icon Sportswire/Newscom; 11 top © J.P. Wilson/Icon SMI/Newscom; 11 bottom © Racheal Grazias/Shutterstock; 12, © Ed Wolfstein/Icon SMI/Newscom; 13, © Focus on Baseball; 14 inset, © AP Photo; 14–15, © Focus on Baseball; 16 top, © Jerry Coli/Dreamstime; 16 bottom, © Nicholc Piccillo/Shutterstock; 17, diagram by Forest Dempsey; 18–19, © SEEPhotos7171/Shutterstock; 19, © Eric Broder Van Dyke/Shutterstock; 20, © Mike Carlson/AP Photo; 21 game, © Lawrence Weselowski, Jr./Dreamstime; 21 hand, © Jaros/Shutterstock; 21 bottom, © Felipe Ponce/Dreamstime; 22, Wikimedia; 23, © Focus on Baseball; 24, © Jerry Coli/Dreamstime; 25 main, © Focus on Baseball; 25 inset, Courtesy Library of Congress; 26, © Focus on Baseball; 27, © Lawrence Weslowski Jr./Dreamstime; 31, © Focus on Baseball

Bearport Publishing Company
Minneapolis, Minnesota
President: Jen Jenson
Director of Product Development: Spencer Brinker
Senior Editor: Allison Juda
Associate Editor: Charly Haley
Designer: Colin O'Dea

Produced by Shoreline Publishing Group LLC
Santa Barbara, California
Designer: Patty Kelley
Editorial Director: James Buckley Jr.

Library of Congress Cataloging-in-Publication Data

Names: Gigliotti, Jim, author.
Title: Baseball : score with STEM! / By Jim Gigliotti.
Description: Minneapolis, Minnesota : Bearport Publishing Company, [2022] | Series: Sports STEM | Includes bibliographical references and index.
Identifiers: LCCN 2021003689 (print) | LCCN 2021003690 (ebook) | ISBN 9781636911762 (library binding) | ISBN 9781636911830 (paperback) | ISBN 9781636911908 (ebook)
Subjects: LCSH: Baseball--Juvenile literature. | Science--Study and teaching--Juvenile literature. | Technology--Study and teaching--Juvenile literature.
Classification: LCC GV867.5 .G54 2022 (print) | LCC GV867.5 (ebook) | DDC 796.357--dc23
LC record available at https://lccn.loc.gov/2021003689
LC ebook record available at https://lccn.loc.gov/2021003690

Copyright © 2022 Bearport Publishing Company. All rights reserved. No part of this publication may be reproduced in whole or in part, stored in any retrieval system, or transmitted in any form or by any means, electronic, mechanical, photocopying, recording, or otherwise, without written permission from the publisher.

For more information, write to Bearport Publishing, 5357 Penn Avenue South, Minneapolis, MN 55419. Printed in the United States of America.

Contents

Baseball and STEM

Los Angeles Angels star Mike Trout digs in at home plate. The pitcher fires a curveball. Trout sees the spin of the ball as it flies toward him. He swings his bat at just the right moment and hits the ball in just the right spot. *Crack!* The ball is going, going, gone! Home run!

Trout may make it look easy, but a lot of hard work—and a little bit of STEM—make for the perfect home run!

SCIENCE: From the rotation on a pitcher's curveball to the **arc** of a long home run, a baseball moves according to the laws of physics.

TECHNOLOGY: Discover how teams use tech like **radar guns** to improve.

ENGINEERING: Stadiums are designed to help fans enjoy games more than ever.

MATH: Information about teams and players is gathered as numbers called **stats**. A winning score is just the beginning!

Science and strength make Mike Trout a star batter.

Curveballs

With every throw, the pitcher tries to get the baseball past a hitter. Sometimes, that means throwing the ball so that it turns as it moves toward the hitter. A curveball follows a straight path, then swoops and dives at the last second. How does a pitcher make the ball move this way?

It's All in the Seams

The **seams** on a baseball rise about 0.03 inches (0.76 mm) above the surface of the ball. That's only about the same thickness as 10 sheets of notebook paper! However, this small height is enough to create **friction** where the air rushes over the seams. The ball's spinning motion combined with friction causes the ball to move to one side or the other. A pitcher controls that movement by the way he grips the seams and spins the ball as he lets it go.

SEAMS

A good curveball might trick a batter into missing the pitch.

The dotted yellow line shows the path a curveball takes. It starts by moving straight, and then it dives down and to the side. A fastball, on other hand, stays on a straight path.

FASTBALL

CURVEBALL

Launch Angle

Hitters use science, too. When a bat hits a ball into the air, an angle is formed between the ground and the ball's path. This angle is called the **launch angle**. If the angle is too high, the opposing team can easily catch a **pop-up** or fly ball. If the angle is too low, the hit can turn into an easily fielded ground ball.

LAUNCH ANGLE

The launch angle changes depending on how the batter swings the bat.

Practice Makes Perfect

Getting the best launch angle takes practice. Pro baseball players use high-speed cameras to help them measure their launch angles. These cameras have shown that an angle between 25 and 35 degrees most often leads to a home run. Knowing this, players try to hit balls within that range as often as they can.

The measurement of how fast a ball comes off the bat is called its exit **velocity**. Adding a high exit velocity to a good launch angle helps players hit home runs even more often! Major League Baseball (MLB) began measuring exit velocity in 2015. By 2020, Giancarlo Stanton had gotten the highest exit velocity in every season!

Giancarlo Stanton

Wide Turn Ahead!

The softball batter smacks the ball into the **outfield gap**. The ball lands and rolls all the way to the wall. Meanwhile, the batter is making a wide turn to hit first base and second base before stopping on third. It's a triple! The shortest distance between two points is a straight line. So, why do batters run in an arc?

The Perfect Arc

Running in a straight line means a player has to slow down to touch a base and turn a corner, and then speed up again to get to the next base. Although the path might be longer, by running in an arc, the player can stay at top speed all the way from first to third.

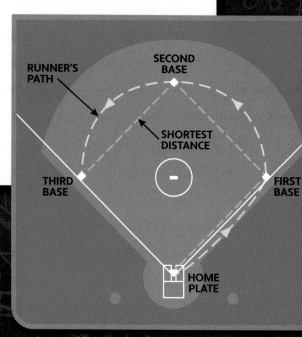

RUNNER'S PATH

SECOND BASE

SHORTEST DISTANCE

THIRD BASE

FIRST BASE

HOME PLATE

A runner pushes off second base during her arc toward third.

When players want to stop, they slide into bases. The friction between the players and the ground slows them down and keeps them from moving past the base.

No Speed Limit

Hitting a fastball is one of the hardest things to do in baseball. These pitches can reach speeds over 100 miles per hour (160.9 kph). Pitchers have always thrown fast, but now they have the technology to measure it. Radar guns track the speed of a ball from a pitcher's hand to home plate.

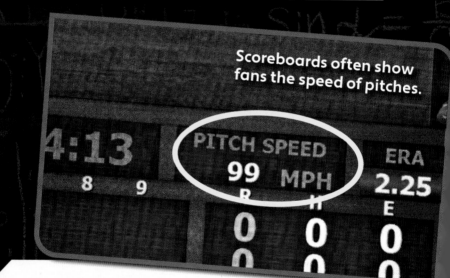

Scoreboards often show fans the speed of pitches.

A Useful Tool

The faster a ball is pitched, the less time a batter has to hit it. Coaches use information about a pitcher's throwing speed to match them up against the best hitters. But it's hard to throw many fast pitches in a ro Coaches can also use radar guns to see if pitches are slowing down, which means the pitcher is getting tire Then, they can bring in a relief pitcher to take over.

The fastest MLB pitch speed ever recorded by a radar gun was 105.1 miles per hour (169.2 kph). Pitcher Aroldis Chapman threw the pitch in 2010.

Tracking Homers

Long-time baseball fans still like to talk about the monster home runs by Mickey Mantle. They say the Yankees star of the 1950s and 1960s once hit a ball 565 feet (172.2 m). Mantle knocked that ball out of the park, but no one knows exactly how far it flew before it landed. Today, technology helps measure the distance a ball travels in every home run hit.

Mickey Mantle

Home runs often fly into the stands—or sometimes even out of the ballpark!

PATH OF BALL

How Far?

Special cameras record every home run hit during professional games. Information from those recordings is combined with a grid that shows exact distances to every part of the stadium. The information is put into an equation, which gives us a number called a projected distance. This is how far the ball would have traveled if something, such as a wall or a fan in the stands, hadn't stopped it.

Ball or Strike?

The pitcher fires the baseball toward home plate, past the batter, and into the catcher's mitt. Everyone waits for the umpire's decision: was it a ball or a strike? Fans watching at home have an advantage. Many televised games feature a video diagram that shows whether a pitch went through the **strike zone**.

An umpire signals that the pitch was a strike.

STRIKE ZONE

The strike zone is the area above home plate between the armpits and knees of a batter.

Steee-rike!

Special cameras in each MLB stadium track every pitch in every game. These cameras capture the speed, **trajectory**, and curve of the baseballs as they fly to home plate. This **data** instantly goes out to TV stations and websites. TV networks use computers to convert the camera information into a **3D** image. It shows viewers the exact path and location of the ball when it crosses home plate.

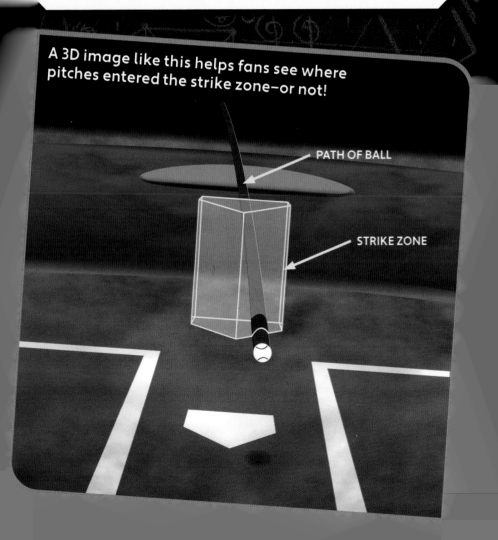

A 3D image like this helps fans see where pitches entered the strike zone—or not!

PATH OF BALL

STRIKE ZONE

No More Rainouts

Thousands of fans gather to watch the game. They fill the seats of the stadium while the players get ready to take the field. Then . . . rain! At most stadiums, rain would probably mean canceling the game. But some stadiums have **retractable** roofs that slowly glide into place. Then, the game is on!

Open and Shut

A retractable roof stays open when the weather is good and can close when the weather is bad. In 2021, seven MLB stadiums had retractable roofs. Each roof works a little differently. Most have two or more enormous moving panels. Powerful motors slide the panels open or closed on steel rails or tracks.

The Marlins stadium in Miami, Florida, has a retractable roof.

PATH OF
RETRACTABLE
ROOF

Because an open roof lets in air and sunshine, retractable roof stadiums can have natural grass fields, just as open stadiums do. Players usually get fewer injuries on grass fields than on **artificial turf.**

More Than a Game

Ballpark engineers have come up with creative new ways to give fans their money's worth at big-league games. At the Tampa Bay Rays' stadium in Saint Petersburg, Florida, fans can touch live cownose rays in a 10,000-gallon (37,854 L) water tank beyond the outfield walls. In Miami, Florida, and in Phoenix, Arizona, fans can swim in a pool while watching a game. Many ballparks have fan zones that include games, rides, and shops.

These rays have a good view of every Rays home game.

There's an App for That

Software engineers are also helping fans by creating apps for game days. Some apps help people find parking places near stadiums. Ticket apps show the view from different seats. **Augmented reality** apps show useful stats, videos, and photos when the viewer just points their phone toward the field!

Jones: 14-4   94 mph

Smith: .354

Augmented reality apps can provide stats in real time.

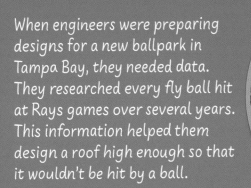

When engineers were preparing designs for a new ballpark in Tampa Bay, they needed data. They researched every fly ball hit at Rays games over several years. This information helped them design a roof high enough so that it wouldn't be hit by a ball.

A Numbers Game

No sport relies on numbers quite as much as baseball. That's been true ever since a newspaper reporter named Henry Chadwick created the first **box score** in 1859. He wanted a way for stats to help tell the story of a game. Today, numbers continue to help show a player's value to their team.

Box scores are broken up into sections that show key stats from each game.

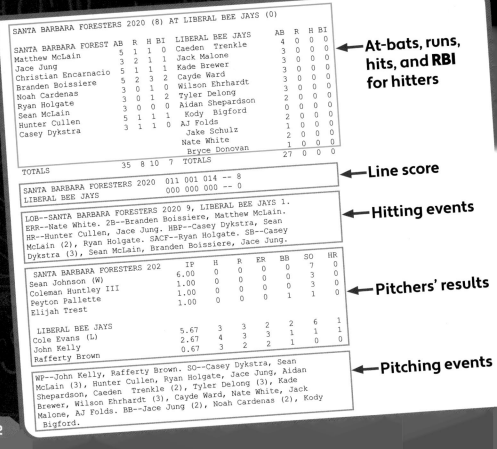

SANTA BARBARA FORESTERS 2020 (8) AT LIBERAL BEE JAYS (0)

SANTA BARBARA FOREST	AB	R	H	BI	LIBERAL BEE JAYS	AB	R	H	BI
Matthew McLain	5	1	1	0	Caeden Trenkle	4	0	0	0
Jace Jung	3	2	1	1	Jack Malone	3	0	0	0
Christian Encarnacio	5	1	1	1	Kade Brewer	3	0	0	0
Branden Boissiere	5	2	3	2	Cayde Ward	3	0	0	0
Noah Cardenas	3	0	1	0	Wilson Ehrhardt	3	0	0	0
Ryan Holgate	3	0	1	2	Tyler Delong	2	0	0	0
Sean McLain	3	0	0	0	Aidan Shepardson	0	0	0	0
Hunter Cullen	5	1	1	1	Kody Bigford	2	0	0	0
Casey Dykstra	3	1	1	0	AJ Folds	1	0	0	0
					Jake Schulz	2	0	0	0
					Nate White	1	0	0	0
					Bryce Donovan	27	0	0	0
TOTALS	35	8	10	7	TOTALS				

At-bats, runs, hits, and **RBI** for hitters

SANTA BARBARA FORESTERS 2020	011 001 014 -- 8
LIBERAL BEE JAYS	000 000 000 -- 0

Line score

LOB--SANTA BARBARA FORESTERS 2020 9, LIBERAL BEE JAYS 1.
ERR--Nate White. 2B--Branden Boissiere, Matthew McLain.
HR--Hunter Cullen, Jace Jung. HBP--Casey Dykstra, Sean
McLain (2), Ryan Holgate. SACF--Ryan Holgate. SB--Casey
Dykstra (3), Sean McLain, Branden Boissiere, Jace Jung.

Hitting events

SANTA BARBARA FORESTERS 202	IP	H	R	ER	BB	SO	HR
Sean Johnson (W)	6.00	0	0	0	0	7	0
Coleman Huntley III	1.00	0	0	0	0	3	0
Peyton Pallette	1.00	0	0	0	0	3	0
Elijah Trest	1.00	0	0	0	1	1	0
LIBERAL BEE JAYS					2	6	1
Cole Evans (L)	5.67	3	3	2	3	1	1
John Kelly	2.67	4	3	3	1	0	0
Rafferty Brown	0.67	3	2	2			

Pitchers' results

WP--John Kelly, Rafferty Brown. SO--Casey Dykstra, Sean
McLain (3), Hunter Cullen, Ryan Holgate, Jace Jung, Aidan
Shepardson, Caeden Trenkle (2), Tyler Delong (3), Kade
Brewer, Wilson Ehrhardt (3), Cayde Ward, Nate White, Jack
Malone, AJ Folds. BB--Jace Jung (2), Noah Cardenas (2), Kody
Bigford.

Pitching events

Mookie Betts's skill at the plate helped the Boston Red Sox win the 2018 World Series.

This Means WAR!

MLB teams also use stats to decide which players would help them create the best lineup on the field. A stat called wins above replacement (WAR) shows how many wins a player gives his team versus a replacement player in the same position. By 2020, the highest single-season WAR among current players was 10.8 by Mookie Betts in 2018.

Hitting Numbers

In pro basketball, a player who only makes 3 shots out of every 10 would soon be out of a job. A football kicker who makes just 4 out of 10 field goals would be cut from the team. In baseball, however, numbers like those describe all-star hitters! Batting is so hard that getting a hit just 3 or 4 times for every 10 times at bat makes you a star.

Batting Average

The most common way to measure a hitter's success is by their batting average. This shows how often a player gets a hit compared to how many times they're at bat. Most MLB players get approximately 1 hit for every 4 times at bat, or an average of .250 (1 ÷ 4). The best hitters have an average of .300 or more. Averages above .350 are reached by only a few great hitters.

A hitter swings and misses!

Hitting a baseball is not easy!

Highest Career Batting
Averages in Baseball History
Ty Cobb .366
Josh Gibson .361
Rogers Hornsby .358
Joe Jackson .356
Lefty O'Doul .349

Ty Cobb

Pitching Numbers

The common way to measure pitchers' performance is by their earned run average (ERA). This stat shows the runs scored against a pitcher for every nine innings of pitching time, not including any runs caused by team errors. A low ERA is good, because it means fewer runs were scored against the pitcher. But teams today are moving past ERA to find other ways to measure pitchers' success.

Keep 'Em Off Base

One of the new ways to size up pitchers is a stat called WHIP, or walks plus hits per inning pitched. This is calculated by adding the number of walks and hits a pitcher has allowed, and then dividing the total by the number of innings pitched. The lower the result, the fewer chances other teams are getting to score.

Jacob deGrom is a good pitcher—he has very low ERA and WHIP stats.

Will this pitch improve the pitcher's stats or the hitter's?

Do the Math!

Ready to do some baseball math? Learn how to calculate four types of stats. Then, do the math to find out which players have the best stats.

Batting Average

A player's batting average is determined by their number of hits divided by their number of at-bats. This stat always shows three places to the right of the decimal point.

1. Which hitter had the best batting average?

PLAYER	HITS	AT-BATS
Freddie Freeman	73	214
DJ LeMahieu	71	195
Juan Soto	54	154

Total Bases

A single means a hitter reached one base. A double means two bases, a triple means three bases, and a home run means the player reached four bases. To find the total bases, use the following formula for each player.

Singles + (doubles x 2) + (triples x 3) + (home runs x 4) = total bases

2. Which hitter had the highest total bases?

PLAYER	SINGLES	DOUBLES	TRIPLES	HOME RUNS
José Abreu	42	15	0	19
Marcell Ozuna	45	14	0	18
Trea Turner	47	15	4	12

Earned Run Average (ERA)

To calculate a pitcher's ERA, multiply the number of earned runs by nine (the number of innings in a game). Then, divide this by the number of innings pitched. All ERA stats include two digits after the decimal point.

3. Which of these star pitchers had the lowest ERA?

PLAYER	EARNED RUNS	INNINGS PITCHED
Shane Bieber	14	77
Gerrit Cole	23	73
Yu Darvish	17	76

WHIP (Walks Plus Hits per Inning Pitched)

WHIP is calculated by adding hits and walks and then dividing the total by the number of innings pitched.

4. Which pitcher had the lower WHIP?

PLAYER	HITS	WALKS	INNINGS PITCHED
Clayton Kershaw	157	39	186
Justin Verlander	180	54	215

Answers:
1. LeMahieu had the best batting average with .364. Soto had .351, and Freeman had .341.
2. Abreu led with 148 total bases [42 + (2 x 15) + 0 + (4 x 19)]. Ozuna was close behind with 145 [45 + (2 x 14) + 0 + (4 x 18)], and Turner got 137 [47 + (2 x 15) + (3 x 4) + (4 x 12) = 137].
3. Bieber had the lowest ERA. His ERA of 1.64 was better than Darvish's 2.01 and Cole's 2.84.
4. Kershaw's 1.054 was better than Verlander's 1.088.

Glossary

arc a path that follows a curve

artificial turf a human-made material that is made to look and feel like grass

augmented reality digital information overlayed on images seen on a digital device

box score a chart showing stats from a baseball game

data information often in the form of numbers

friction the resistance to motion when two things rub against one another

launch angle the angle made by the path of the ball after being hit by the bat

outfield gap the open areas to the left and right of the center fielder

pop-up a batted ball that flies high up in the air but does not go far into the field

radar guns handheld devic[e] that measure the speed of moving objects

RBI short for runs batted ir[n] a stat that records when a player helps a teammate s[core] a run

retractable able to pull ba[ck] or inside

seams the raised stitches [on] baseball

stats short for statistics; information stated as num[bers]

strike zone an area over home plate that pitches m[ust] pass through to be called strikes

3D short for three-dimensional; a way t[o] show the real shape of obje[cts] on a flat surface

trajectory the path on whi[ch] an object travels

velocity the distance something travels in a set amount of time

Read More

Clark, Aimee. *STEM in Baseball & Softball (Connecting STEM and Sports).* Broomall, PA: Mason Crest, 2020.

Helget, Nicole Lea. *Full STEAM Baseball: Science, Technology, Engineering, Arts, and Mathematics of the Game (Full STEAM Sports).* North Mankato, MN: Capstone Press, 2019.

Ventura, Marne. *STEM in the World Series (STEM in the Greatest Sports Events).* Minneapolis: Abdo Publishing, 2020.

Learn More Online

1. Go to **www.factsurfer.com**

2. Enter "**STEM Baseball**" into the search box.

3. Click on the cover of this book to see a list of websites.

Index

About the Author

Jim Gigliotti has written more than 100 books, many of them on sports, for young readers. Before becoming a freelance writer, he worked for the University of Southern California, the Los Angeles Dodgers, and the National Football League.